HE FIGHTS
FOR YOU

HE FIGHTS FOR YOU

40 Promises for Everyday Battles

Max Lucado
and Andrea Lucado

Thomas Nelson
Since 1798

NASHVILLE   MEXICO CITY   RIO DE JANEIRO

Published in Nashville, Tennessee, by Thomas Nelson. Thomas Nelson is a registered trademark of HarperCollins Christian Publishing, Inc.

Thomas Nelson titles may be purchased in bulk for educational, business, fundraising, or sales promotional use. For information, please e-mail SpecialMarkets@ThomasNelson.com.

Unless otherwise noted, Scripture quotations are taken from the New King James Version®. © 1982 by Thomas Nelson. Used by permission. All rights reserved.

Other Scripture references are from the following sources: English Standard Version (ESV). © 2001 by Crossway Bibles, a division of Good News Publishers. King James Version (KJV). *The Message* (MSG) by Eugene H. Peterson. © 1993, 1994, 1995, 1996, 2000, 2001, 2002. Used by permission of NavPress Publishing Group. All rights reserved. New Century Version® (NCV). © 2005 by Thomas Nelson. Used by permission. All rights reserved. Holy Bible, New International Version®, NIV® (NIV). Copyright © 1973, 1978, 1984, 2011 by Biblica, Inc.™ Used by permission of Zondervan. All rights reserved worldwide. www.zondervan.com.

ISBN: 978-0-7180-3790-1

Printed in the United States of America

15 16 17 18 19 RRD 6 5 4 3 2 1

WALK CIRCLES
AROUND YOUR
JERICHO

Here is what you need to know about the walls of Jericho. They were immense. They wrapped around the city like a suit of armor, two concentric circles of stone rising a total of forty feet above the ground. Impenetrable.

Here is what you need to know about Jericho's inhabitants. They were ferocious and barbaric. They withstood all sieges and repelled all invaders. They were guilty of child sacrifice. "They even burn their sons and daughters as sacrifices to their gods!" (Deut. 12:31 NCV). They were a Bronze-age version of the gestapo, ruthless tyrants on the plains of Canaan.[1] Until the day Joshua showed up.

Until the day his army marched in. Until the day the bricks cracked and the boulders broke. Until the day everything shook—the stones of the walls, the knees of the king, the molars of the soldiers. The untoppleable fortress met the unstoppable force.

Mighty Jericho crumbled.

But here is what you need to know about Joshua. He didn't bring the walls down. Joshua's soldiers never swung a hammer. His men never dislodged a brick. They never rammed a door or pried loose a stone. The shaking, quaking, rumbling, and tumbling of the thick, impervious walls? God did that for them.

God will do that for you. Your Jericho is your fear. Your Jericho is your anger, bitterness, or prejudice. Your insecurity about the future. Your guilt about the past. Your negativity, anxiety, and proclivity to criticize, overanalyze, or compartmentalize. Your Jericho is any attitude or mind-set that keeps you from joy, peace, or rest.

Jericho.

It stands between you and your Glory Days. It mocks you and tells you to take your dreams back to the wilderness. It stands like an ogre on the bridge of progress. It is big; it is evil. It blocks your way. And its walls must fall. To live in the Promised Land, you must face your Jericho.

It's not always easy. Every level of inheritance requires a disinheritance from the devil. Satan must be moved off before the saint can move in. Joshua told his people to "go in to possess the land which the LORD your God is giving you to possess" (Josh. 1:11). The verb translated *possess* means "to occupy" (by driving out previous tenants, and possessing in their place).[2] Satan won't leave without a fight. He will resist. He will push back. But he will not win. Why? Because God has already declared that you are the victor. Satan, defanged and defeated at Calvary, has no authority over you.

God's word to Joshua is God's word to us: "Be strong and of good courage" (1:6). Do not heed your fear. Do not cower before your woes. Take the land God has given you to possess.

"And the LORD said to Joshua: 'See! I have given Jericho into your hand, its king, and the mighty men of valor'" (6:2).

God did not say, "Joshua, take the city."

God said, "Joshua, receive the city I have taken."

Joshua did not go forth hoping to win. He knew that God had already won.

———

The same can be said about you and your challenge. God does not say, "Bob, break your bad habit."

He says, "Bob, I have broken the bad habits of your life. Receive the blessing of my victory."

Remember, you are a coheir with Christ. Every attribute of Jesus is at your disposal. Was Jesus victorious? Did he overcome sin and death? Yes! Will you be victorious? Can you overcome sin and death? Yes! The question is not, will you overcome? It is, *when* will you overcome? Life will always bring challenges. But God will always give strength to face them.

Things are different in the Promised Land. Hang-ups and addictions do not have the last word. Today's problem is not necessarily tomorrow's problem. Don't incarcerate yourself by assuming it is. Resist self-labeling. "I'm just a worrier." "Gossip is my weakness." "My dad was a drinker, and I guess I'll carry on the tradition."

Stop that! These words create alliances with the devil. They grant him access to your spirit. It is not God's will that you live a defeated, marginalized, unhappy, and weary life. Turn a deaf ear to the old voices and make new choices. "The lines have fallen to me in pleasant places; yes, I have a good inheritance" (Ps. 16:6). Live out of your inheritance, not your circumstance.

God has already promised a victory. And he has provided weapons for the fight.

I can picture the soldiers perking up as Joshua, their commander, announces, "It is time to take Jericho!"

"Great!" they reply. "We have our ladders and ropes!"

"We will scale the walls!"

"Our spears are sharpened, and our swords are polished!"

"Which side do we attack first?"

Joshua looks at his men and says, "Well, God has a different strategy." The general outlines the most unlikely of attacks. "Take up the ark of the covenant, and let seven priests bear seven trumpets of rams' horns before the ark of the LORD" (Josh. 6:6).

Joshua commands soldiers to march before and behind the priests. He tells the priests to blow the trumpets continually as they walk around the city once a day. As for the rest of the people? "You shall not shout or make any noise with your voice, nor shall a word proceed out of your mouth, until the day I say to you, 'Shout!' Then you shall shout" (v. 10).

Wait a minute. No war cry? No hand-to-hand combat? No flashing swords, flying spears, battering rams, or catapults? Just priests, rams' horns, marching, and silence? Joshua has at least forty thousand soldiers at his command, and he tells them to be quiet and watch?

What kind of warfare is this?

Spiritual warfare. Every battle, ultimately, is a spiritual battle. Every conflict is a contest with Satan and his forces. Paul urged us to stand "against the wiles of the devil" (Eph. 6:11). The Greek word he used for "wiles" is *methodia*, from which we get our English word *method*.[3] Satan is not passive or fair. He is active and deceptive. He has designs and strategies. Consequently, we need a strategy as well. For that reason "though we walk in the flesh, we do not war according to the flesh. For the weapons of our warfare are not carnal but mighty in God for pulling down strongholds" (2 Cor. 10:3–4).

Just as Jericho was a stronghold in Canaan, we have strongholds in our lives. The apostle Paul used the term to describe a mind-set or attitude.

"The weapons of our warfare are . . . mighty in God for pulling down *strongholds*, casting down arguments and every high thing that exalts itself against the knowledge of God" (vv. 4–5, emphasis mine). The apostle defined a stronghold as an argument or high thing that "exalts itself against the knowledge of God." It is a conviction, outlook, or belief that attempts to interfere with truth.

Other translations describe a stronghold as

- "imaginations" (KJV),
- "pretension" (NIV),
- "lofty opinion" (ESV),
- "warped philosophies" (MSG).

A stronghold is a false premise that denies God's promise. It "sets itself up against the knowledge of God" (v. 5 NIV). It seeks to eclipse our discovery of God. It attempts to magnify the problem and minimize God's ability to solve it.

Does a stronghold have a strong hold on you? Do you see nothing but Jericho? Do you feel nothing but despair? Do you think thoughts of defeat? Do you speak the language of impossibility?

God could never forgive me. (the stronghold of guilt)

I could never forgive that person. (the stronghold of resentment)

Bad things always happen to me. (the stronghold of self-pity)

I have to be in charge. (the stronghold of pride)

I don't deserve to be loved. (the stronghold of rejection)

I'll never recover. (the stronghold of defeat)

I must be good, or God will reject me. (the stronghold of performance)

I'm only as good as I look. (the stronghold of appearance)

My value equals my possessions. (the stronghold of materialism)

Most Christians don't recognize strongholds.[4] They live in the shadow of these joy-sucking Jerichos.

But we don't have to be among them. Our weapons are from God and have "divine power to demolish strongholds" (v. 4 NIV).

Isn't that what we want? We long to see our strongholds demolished, turned into rubble once and for all, forever and ever, *ka-boom!* We long to see Jericho brought to the ground. How does this happen?

By keeping God in the center.

The ark of the covenant was the symbol of the Lord's presence. Joshua placed the ark in the middle of the procession. Every activity orbited around God. We don't attack our Jericho with anger, blame casting, or finger-pointing. No, we keep God center stage, using the weapons of worship, Scripture, and prayer. We employ every tool God offers: hymns, songs, communion, Scripture memorization, and petition. We turn off the TV and open the Bible more. We remember Jesus' promise: "I am with you always" (Matt. 28:20). We worry less, pray always. We even blast our version of a ram's horn.

Ram's horn?

The Hebrews used two instruments: the silver trumpet and the ram's horn. The silver trumpet was used to call the people to assemble (Num. 10:2). The ram's horn celebrated a battle already won. When Abraham displayed his willingness to give up his son Isaac as an offering, God stopped him and provided a ram. The ram's horn reminds us of God's sovereign generosity. God gave Abraham a ram of deliverance. God told Joshua to fill the air with sounds of ram's horn victory.

And, curiously, he told the people to keep quiet. "Don't say a word" (Josh. 6:10 NCV). No chitchat. No opinion giving or second-guessing. No whining or chatting. Keep your mouth shut and the trumpets loud.

Imagine the reaction of the Canaanites as Joshua's army marched circles around them. The first day they mocked the Hebrews. The second day they scoffed again but not as loudly. By the fourth and fifth days, the enemy had grown silent. *What are these Hebrews up to?* they wondered. On the sixth day the Canaanites were dry mouthed and wide eyed as the Hebrews made their round. The people of Jericho had never fought a battle like this.

Just as challenging is your battle with your archenemy, the devil. He has held this stronghold in your life for years. You've tried everything to overcome it: renewed discipline, self-help books, pop culture gurus. Nothing helps. But now you come in God's power with God center stage, Jesus in your heart, angels in front and back. You come, not with hope of a possible victory, but with assurance of complete victory.

March like a Promised Land conqueror. Blast your ram's horn. Sing songs of redemption, and declare scriptures of triumph. Marinate your mind with the declaration of Jesus, "It is finished!"

(John 19:30), and the announcement of the angels, "He is not here; for He is risen" (Matt. 28:6). Personalize the proclamations of Paul: "We are more than conquerors through [Christ]" (Rom. 8:37), and "I can do all things through Christ" (Phil. 4:13). As you do, the demons will begin to scatter. They have no choice but to leave.

Sometime back a mother asked me to pray for her eight-year-old son. He was troubled by a constant barrage of images and scary visions. He saw people behind cars and in shadows. The images left him withdrawn and timid. They even took his sleep at night.

On the day we met he appeared defeated. His smile was gone. While his other siblings were confident and happy, there was no joy in his face. His eyes often filled with tears, and he clung to his mother.

She had taken him to doctors, but nothing had helped. Would I be willing to pray for him?

I told the young boy what I've been telling you. That the devil has no authority over his life. That the real battles are fought in the mind. That God will help us take every thought captive.

I told him about the spiritual weapons of worship, Scripture, and prayer and urged him to memorize a Bible verse and quote it each time the fearful thoughts came to mind. I gave him a tool. "Reach up with your hand," I urged, "and grab the thought and throw it in the trash. And as quickly as you do that, replace it with a verse of Scripture." We then anointed him with oil and prayed.

Five days later his mother reported great progress. "Since last week the images are gone; he is no longer seeing them. He is doing well in school, and he is enjoying reading the book of Genesis. God gave us Psalm 25:5, 'Lead me in Your truth and teach me, for You are the God of my salvation; on You I wait all the day.' He recites this verse nightly. I believe this has brought him closer to Christ. He uses the strategy of throwing the fearful thoughts away in the trash can. He said when he tried to throw them away, his head would hurt. I asked, 'What made them go away?' He smiled and said, 'I know God made them go away.'"[5]

Another Jericho bites the dust.

"Yell a loud *no* to the Devil and watch him scamper" (James 4:7 MSG). He will retreat. He *must* retreat. He is not allowed in the place where God is praised. Just keep praising and walking.

"But, Max, I've been walking a long time," you say.

Yes, it seems like it. It must have seemed that way to the Hebrews too. Joshua did not tell them how many trips they would have to make around the city. God told Joshua that the walls would fall on the seventh day, but Joshua didn't tell the people. They just kept walking.

Our Joshua didn't tell us either. Through the pen of Paul, Jesus urges us to "be steadfast, immovable, always abounding in the work of the Lord, knowing that your labor is not in vain in the Lord" (1 Cor. 15:58).

Keep walking. For all you know this may be the day the walls come down. You may be only steps from a moment like this.

On the seventh day . . . they rose early, about the dawning of the day, and marched around the city seven times in the same manner . . . And the seventh time it happened, when the priests blew the trumpets, that Joshua said to the people: "Shout, for the LORD has given you the city! . . . "

So the people shouted when the priests blew the trumpets. And it happened when the people heard the sound of the trumpet, and the people shouted with a great shout, that the wall fell down flat. Then the people . . . took the city. (Josh. 6:15–16, 20)

The very walls that kept them out became stepping-stones onto which they could climb.

By the way, a great shaking is coming for this world too. Our Joshua, Jesus, will give the signal, and a trumpet will blast. He will reclaim every spoil and repel, once and for all, each demon. He will do again what he did in Canaan.

Until he does, keep marching and believing. Defeat your strongholds with the spiritual weapons of worship, Scripture, and prayer. Move from false premises to God's promises.

It's just a matter of time before your Jericho comes down.

I

WORSHIP

My sin—oh, the bliss of this glorious thought—
My sin—not in part but the whole,
Is nailed to the cross, and I bear it no more,
Praise the Lord, praise the Lord, O my soul!

"IT IS WELL WITH MY SOUL" BY HORATIO G. SPAFFORD

SCRIPTURE

But thanks be to God, who gives us the victory
through our Lord Jesus Christ.

1 CORINTHIANS 15:57

PRAYER

Dear God, thank you for the victory I have in Christ. Because of him, my sin is no more and I am eternally grateful for that. It is truly a "glorious thought" to know that all of my shame was covered at the cross, and that I can walk forward today not wondering if I am saved, but knowing that I am, because the victory is yours. In Jesus' name, amen.

2

WORSHIP

Glory to the King of angels,
Glory to the church's King,
Glory to the King of nations!
Heaven and earth, your praises bring;
Glory, glory, glory, glory,
To the King of glory bring!

"GLORY BE TO GOD THE FATHER" BY HORATIUS BONAR

SCRIPTURE

For by Him all things were created that are in
heaven and that are on earth, visible and invisible,
whether thrones or dominions or principalities or
powers. All things were created through Him and
for Him.

COLOSSIANS 1:16

PRAYER

*Dear God, all glory, honor, and power are yours. You created
the heavens and the earth. You know your creation, and you
care about your children deeply. I will never fully understand the
greatness of your power or the depth of your love. In Jesus' name,
amen.*

3

WORSHIP

Praise the name of the LORD!
Blessed be the name of the LORD
From this time forth and evermore!
From the rising of the sun to its going down
The LORD's name is to be praised.

PSALM 113:1–3

SCRIPTURE

"They will fight against you, but they shall not prevail against you. For I am with you," says the LORD, "to deliver you."

JEREMIAH 1:19

PRAYER

Almighty Father, you have promised to deliver me from my enemies, and you keep your promises. I praise you for the works you have done, the works you are doing, and the works you will do. Thank you for fighting for me. Thank you for being near to me. In Christ's name I pray, amen.

4

WORSHIP

Oh, how great is Your goodness,
Which You have laid up for those who fear You,
Which You have prepared for those who trust in You
In the presence of the sons of men!

PSALM 31:19

SCRIPTURE

And let us run with endurance the race that is
set before us, looking unto Jesus, the author and
finisher of our faith, who for the joy that was
set before Him endured the cross, despising the
shame, and has sat down at the right hand of the
throne of God.

HEBREWS 12:1–2

PRAYER

*Dear Father, how great is your goodness toward me. You sent
your Son, who won the victory over death and sin, for me. In him
I have hope. In him I have victory. In Christ's name I pray, amen.*

5

WORSHIP

The LORD is my light and my salvation;
Whom shall I fear?
The LORD is the strength of my life;
Of whom shall I be afraid?

PSALM 27:1

SCRIPTURE

Have I not commanded you? Be strong and of
good courage; do not be afraid, nor be dismayed,
for the LORD your God is with you wherever you go.

JOSHUA 1:9

PRAYER

Father, with you by my side, I don't need to be afraid. No matter what comes my way, you have promised to be my strength and to give me courage. Because of you, I have peace. Because of you, I know which direction to go. Thank you for being my light and my salvation. In Jesus' name, amen.

6

WORSHIP

Great love of God, come in!
Wellspring of heavenly peace;
Thou Living Water, come!
Spring up, and never cease.

"O LOVE THAT CASTS OUT FEAR" BY HORATIUS BONAR

SCRIPTURE

If anyone thirsts, let him come to Me and drink.
He who believes in Me, as the Scripture has said,
out of his heart will flow rivers of living water.

JOHN 7:37–38

PRAYER

Dear God, you give me true life. Nothing on this earth satisfies like you do. May I love others as you have loved me, forgive others as you have forgiven me, and accept others as you have accepted me. In Jesus' name, amen.

7

WORSHIP

Christ, above all glory seated!
King triumphant, strong to save!
Dying, Thou hast death defeated;
Buried, Thou hast spoiled the grave.

"CHRIST, ABOVE ALL GLORY SEATED" BY JOHN

B. DYKES AND JAMES R. WOODFORD

SCRIPTURE

I am persuaded that neither death nor life . . . nor things present nor things to come, nor height nor depth . . . shall be able to separate us from the love of God which is in Christ Jesus our Lord.

ROMANS 8:38–39

PRAYER

Almighty God, nothing can separate me from your love. Through Christ I can have a personal relationship with you. His death tore the veil that separated you and me, and his resurrection restored us. I praise you, and I thank you for the gift of your Son. In your Son's name, amen.

8

WORSHIP

A mighty fortress is our God, a bulwark never
    failing;
Our helper He, amid the flood of mortal ills
    prevailing.

"A MIGHTY FORTRESS IS OUR GOD" BY MARTIN LUTHER

SCRIPTURE

The LORD is my rock and my fortress and my
    deliverer;
The God of my strength, in whom I will trust;
My shield and the horn of my salvation,
My stronghold and my refuge.

2 SAMUEL 22:2–3

PRAYER

*God, you are my rock and my refuge. When I experience highs
and lows, you are steady and constant. I can run to you when I
need shelter and protection. My salvation is in you, and that will
never change. In Jesus' name, amen.*

9

WORSHIP

The LORD is gracious and full of compassion,
Slow to anger and great in mercy.
The LORD is good to all,
And His tender mercies are over all His works.

PSALM 145:8–9

SCRIPTURE

He will again have compassion on us,
And will subdue our iniquities.
You will cast all our sins
Into the depths of the sea.

MICAH 7:19

PRAYER

Father, you are good. You cast my sin as far as the east is from the west. You extend grace and mercy that I do not deserve. I am so grateful for the transforming power of your kindness and love. May I live confidently in the promise of your forgiveness. In Christ's name, amen.

10

WORSHIP

Oh, that men would give thanks to the LORD for His
    goodness,
And for His wonderful works to the children of men!
For He satisfies the longing soul,
And fills the hungry soul with goodness.

PSALM 107:8–9

SCRIPTURE

Blessed are those who hunger and thirst for
    righteousness,
For they shall be filled.

MATTHEW 5:6

PRAYER

Dear Father, only you can satisfy the longing in my soul. You fill me with love, joy, and hope, and those are the gifts that last. The things of this earth leave me unsatisfied, but true life is found in you. Thank you for your goodness. In your name I pray, amen.

II

WORSHIP

God, you are worthy.
Your love never ends.
God, you are mighty.
On you, I can depend.

God, you are righteous.
Your children look to you.
God, you are good.
You are all that is holy, pure, and true.

ANDREA LUCADO

SCRIPTURE

Instead of your shame you shall have double honor,
And instead of confusion they shall rejoice in their
   portion.
Therefore in their land they shall possess double;
Everlasting joy shall be theirs.

ISAIAH 61:7

PRAYER

Almighty God, you took away my sin, and I come before your throne with confidence because of Jesus. I praise you for the blessings you have given and the ones you will give. Your love and faithfulness endure forever. In Jesus' name, amen.

12

WORSHIP

Through the LORD's mercies we are not consumed,
Because His compassions fail not.
They are new every morning;
Great is Your faithfulness.
"The LORD is my portion," says my soul,
"Therefore I hope in Him!"

LAMENTATIONS 3:22–24

SCRIPTURE

But God, who is rich in mercy, because of His great love with which He loved us, even when we were dead in trespasses, made us alive together with Christ.

EPHESIANS 2:4–5

PRAYER

Dear God, you are rich in mercy. Your mercies are new every morning. They sustain me and give me hope. Even when I wake up knowing a hard day is ahead, your Word promises that you will give me strength and peace. I am so grateful for that assurance. It's in your name I pray, amen.

13

WORSHIP

Victory, victory, victory in Jesus!
Sing His overcoming blood, sing the grace that frees
us;
Ring it out more boldly, song of faith and cheer,
Till the whole wide world shall hear.

"VICTORY IN JESUS" BY ELIZA E. HEWITT

SCRIPTURE

And he shall say to them, "Hear, O Israel: Today
you are on the verge of battle with your enemies.
Do not let your heart faint, do not be afraid, and
do not tremble or be terrified because of them; for
the LORD your God is He who goes with you, to
fight for you against your enemies, to save you."

DEUTERONOMY 20:3–4

PRAYER

*Dear Father, as you delivered the Israelites, so will you deliver me.
The battles I face are yours. The victory is already won. You are
with me. You fight for me. You save me, and because of this, I do
not have to fear. In Christ I pray, amen.*

14

WORSHIP

I will love You, O LORD, my strength.
I will call upon the LORD, who is worthy to be
   praised;
So shall I be saved from my enemies.

PSALM 18:1, 3

SCRIPTURE

The LORD is my strength and song,
And He has become my salvation;
He is my God, and I will praise Him;
My father's God, and I will exalt Him.

EXODUS 15:2

PRAYER

*Heavenly Father, you are my strength and my song, my salvation
and my deliverer. I praise you because you are worthy to be
praised. I depend on you for strength each hour of each day. When
I struggle, you carry me. Thank you for being my rock and my
fortress. In Jesus' name, amen.*

15

WORSHIP

Oh, sing to the LORD a new song!
For He has done marvelous things;
His right hand and His holy arm have gained Him
the victory.

PSALM 98:1

SCRIPTURE

Blessed be the God and Father of our Lord Jesus
Christ, who has blessed us with every spiritual
blessing in the heavenly places in Christ.

EPHESIANS 1:3

PRAYER

*Dear God, you have done amazing things in my life. You have
blessed me beyond what I could have imagined. In the face of
difficulty or sadness, I always have something to be grateful for.
I always have a reason to praise you. Your glory, grace, and love
overcome the darkness, and I declare your victory. I am so grateful
that I belong to you, God. In Jesus' name, amen.*

16

WORSHIP

Salvation! O Thou bleeding Lamb,
To Thee the praise belongs;
Salvation shall inspire our hearts,
And dwell upon our tongues.

"SALVATION! O THE JOYFUL SOUND!" BY ISAAC WATTS

SCRIPTURE

But we all, with unveiled face, beholding as
in a mirror the glory of the Lord, are being
transformed into the same image from glory to
glory, just as by the Spirit of the Lord.

2 CORINTHIANS 3:18

PRAYER

Father God, the author of my salvation, I praise you and I thank you. Every day you transform me more into the image of your Son. You have won the battle over sin and are my hope for heaven and all of eternity. In the name of Christ I pray, amen.

17

WORSHIP

I will sing of your grace,
For there is no other song worth singing.

I will dance a dance of praise,
Because there is no other dance worth dancing.

I will write of your unending love and mercy,
For there is no other story worth writing.

ANDREA LUCADO

SCRIPTURE

For by grace you have been saved through faith,
and that not of yourselves; it is the gift of God, not
of works, lest anyone should boast.

EPHESIANS 2:8–9

PRAYER

Heavenly Father, grace, and your grace alone, sustains me throughout this life. I cannot make it in my own power, but my weakness shows off your strength. Time and again you prove that all power and glory and honor are yours. In Jesus' name I pray, amen.

18

WORSHIP

Now I know that the LORD saves His anointed;
He will answer him from His holy heaven
With the saving strength of His right hand.
Some trust in chariots, and some in horses;
But we will remember the name of the LORD our God.

PSALM 20:6–7

SCRIPTURE

Let not your heart be troubled; you believe in God,
believe also in Me.

JOHN 14:1

PRAYER

*Jesus, when I am anxious and confused, help me to trust in you.
The things of this world are like shifting sand, but your love and
faithfulness are steady and unending. They are greater than any
superficial hope this world has to offer. You are my God, and I am
your child. In your name, amen.*

19

WORSHIP

Majestic sweetness sits enthroned
Upon the Savior's brow;
His head with radiant glories crowned,
His lips with grace o'erflow,
His lips with grace o'erflow.

"MAJESTIC SWEETNESS SITS ENTHRONED"
BY SAMUEL STENNETT

SCRIPTURE

If God is for us, who can be against us? He who
did not spare His own Son, but delivered Him up
for us all, how shall He not with Him also freely
give us all things?

ROMANS 8:31–32

PRAYER

*God, you will save me from my strongholds. Because you are for
me, nothing can be against me. Thank you for fighting spiritual
battles for me. Thank you for giving me your victory so that I can
live with confidence. In the precious name of your Son, amen.*

20

WORSHIP

But You are holy,
Enthroned in the praises of Israel.
Our fathers trusted in You;
They trusted, and You delivered them.
They cried to You, and were delivered;
They trusted in You, and were not ashamed.

PSALM 22:3–5

SCRIPTURE

Yes, we had the sentence of death in ourselves,
that we should not trust in ourselves but in God
who raises the dead, who delivered us from so
great a death, and does deliver us; in whom we
trust that He will still deliver us.

2 CORINTHIANS 1:9–10

PRAYER

Dear God, no problem is too big or enemy too strong for you. You have always saved me, and you will continue to deliver me from sin and strongholds. Because of your faithfulness, I trust in you. In your name I pray, amen.

21

WORSHIP

Blessed be the LORD my Rock,
Who trains my hands for war,
And my fingers for battle—
My lovingkindness and my fortress,
My high tower and my deliverer,
My shield and the One in whom I take refuge.

PSALM 144:1–2

SCRIPTURE

Yet in all these things we are more than
conquerors through Him who loved us.

ROMANS 8:37

PRAYER

Dear God, you are my rock. You have made me more than a conqueror in Jesus' name. It's easy to feel overwhelmed in this life, but I know that you will win every battle. I trust that you will protect me at all times. Because of your lovingkindness, I am saved. In your name I pray, amen.

22

WORSHIP

Let the whole creation cry: Alleluia!
Glory to the Lord on high! Alleluia!
Heav'n and earth, awake and sing: Alleluia!
God is good and therefore king! Alleluia!

"LET THE WHOLE CREATION CRY" BY STOPFORD A. BROOKE

SCRIPTURE

You alone are the LORD;
You have made heaven,
The heaven of heavens, with all their host,
The earth and everything on it,
The seas and all that is in them,
And You preserve them all.
The host of heaven worships You.

NEHEMIAH 9:6

PRAYER

Almighty God, you created the heavens and the earth and everything in them. How could anything stand against you? You've created every mountain and orchestrated each sunset. And you hold me in the same hands that hold the universe. I'm humbled and comforted. Thank you for caring about every detail of my life. In Jesus' name, amen.

23

WORSHIP

The pow'r of God is just the same today,
It doesn't matter what the people say;
Whatever God has promised
He's able to perform:
And the power of God is just the same today.

"THE POWER OF GOD" BY FREDERICK A. GRAVES

SCRIPTURE

Then He arose and rebuked the wind, and said to the sea, "Peace, be still!" And the wind ceased and there was a great calm.

MARK 4:39

PRAYER

Heavenly Father, I am so quick to forget your power and your authority. Remind me that you are the God who calms the wind and the waves. You are the God who is worshipped by man and also by nature. The storms that I face are nothing compared to your strength. You bring peace and calm with a single word. All creation obeys you, and all creation worships you. In Christ's name, amen.

24

WORSHIP

We will rejoice in your salvation,
And in the name of our God we will set up our
    banners!
May the LORD fulfill all your petitions.
Now I know that the LORD saves His anointed;
He will answer him from His holy heaven
With the saving strength of His right hand.

PSALM 20:5–6

SCRIPTURE

Ask, and it will be given to you; seek, and you
will find; knock, and it will be opened to you.
For everyone who asks receives, and he who seeks
finds, and to him who knocks it will be opened.

MATTHEW 7:7–8

PRAYER

*Father, you have given me the victory. All I have to do is ask, and
I will receive it. You are quick to open the door when I knock.
Thank you for always being present in my life and never turning
me away. Thank you for your steadfast love. In your name I pray
this, amen.*

25

WORSHIP

All hail the power of Jesus' name! Let angels
    prostrate fall;
Bring forth the royal diadem, and crown Him Lord
    of all.
Let every tribe and every tongue before Him
    prostrate fall
And shout in universal song the crowned Lord of all.

"ALL HAIL THE POWER OF JESUS' NAME"
BY EDWARD PERRONET

SCRIPTURE

Finally, my brethren, be strong in the Lord and in
the power of His might.

EPHESIANS 6:10

PRAYER

*Father, I worship you along with the angels and all of creation.
You are Lord of all, yet you are near to me, especially in times
of heartbreak. When I am broken, be near me. Give me your
strength and hold me up with your might. Thank you for caring
for the people of this world from every tribe and tongue. In Jesus'
name, amen.*

26

WORSHIP

We praise Thee, O God!
For the Son of Thy love,
For Jesus who died,
And is now gone above.
We praise Thee, O God!
For Thy Spirit of light,
Who has shown us our Savior,
And scattered our night.

"REVIVE US AGAIN" BY WILLIAM P. MACKAY

SCRIPTURE

Now to Him who is able to do exceedingly
abundantly above all that we ask or think,
according to the power that works in us, to Him
be glory in the church by Christ Jesus to all
generations, forever and ever. Amen.

EPHESIANS 3:20–21

PRAYER

*My God, there is no limit to your power and your ability. What
seems impossible to me is more than possible with you, and with
your Spirit in me, I can overcome. I am victorious in Christ
because of your goodness. Thank you for this victory. In Jesus'
name, amen.*

WORSHIP

The one who has won the battle,
He is who I praise.
The one who has gone before,
His banner will I raise.

The one who is only good,
He is who I look to.
The one who sits on high,
His strength will pull me through.

ANDREA LUCADO

SCRIPTURE

For I, the LORD your God, will hold your right
    hand,
Saying to you, "Fear not, I will help you."

ISAIAH 41:13

PRAYER

Dear God, you are always there when I cry for help. You've never left my side. Thank you. Sometimes my focus strays. Help me to keep my eyes on you, the one true God. Your power and strength pull me out of the pit, and I love you for that. In Jesus' name, amen.

28

WORSHIP

I will praise You, O LORD, among the peoples,
And I will sing praises to You among the nations.
For Your mercy is great above the heavens,
And Your truth reaches to the clouds.

PSALM 108:3–4

SCRIPTURE

But according to His mercy He saved us, through
the washing of regeneration and renewing of
the Holy Spirit, whom He poured out on us
abundantly through Jesus Christ our Savior.

TITUS 3:5–6

PRAYER

*Father, nothing compares to your great mercy. I don't deserve your
grace, but you give it to me freely and abundantly. Through the
gift of the Holy Spirit, I can live in the truth of your never-ending
mercies and can live in your victory. In Christ I pray, amen.*

29

WORSHIP

For I will not trust in my bow,
Nor shall my sword save me.
But You have saved us from our enemies,
And have put to shame those who hated us.
In God we boast all day long,
And praise Your name forever.

PSALM 44:6–8

SCRIPTURE

Thus says the LORD to you: "Do not be afraid nor dismayed because of this great multitude, for the battle is not yours, but God's."

2 CHRONICLES 20:15

PRAYER

Dear Jesus, this is my surrender. I lay down my earthly weapons. I lay down my striving. I lay down all of my attempts to win my own battles. I cannot win on my own. But you can, and the battle belongs to you. I surrender all to you. I boast only about your goodness, love, and strength. In Christ I pray, amen.

30

WORSHIP

All creatures of our God and King
Lift up your voice and with us sing,
Alleluia! Alleluia!
Thou burning sun with golden beam,
Thou silver moon with softer gleam!

O praise Him! O praise Him!
Alleluia! Alleluia! Alleluia!

"ALL CREATURES OF OUR GOD AND
KING" BY FRANCIS OF ASSISI

SCRIPTURE

After these things I heard a loud voice of a great
multitude in heaven, saying, "Alleluia! Salvation
and glory and honor and power belong to the
Lord our God!"

REVELATION 19:1

PRAYER

*Father, I look forward to the day that all creation will declare your
name and your glory. You deserve all praise, and you created me
to worship you. Today, let me live in the spirit of worship. Let the
first words that I speak in every situation be praise to you. In your
name I pray, amen.*

31

WORSHIP

O LORD, our Lord,
How excellent is Your name in all the earth,
Who have set Your glory above the heavens!

PSALM 8:1

SCRIPTURE

And lo, I am with you always, even to the end of
the age.

MATTHEW 28:20

PRAYER

Dear God, there's no distance I could go that would take me from your love. There is nothing I could do that would make you love me any less. You not only promised me your presence in this moment, but you also promised me your presence until the end of time. When nothing else in my world seems to last, your love does, and it will, forever. Thank you, Father. It's in your name I pray, amen.

32

WORSHIP

But I have trusted in Your mercy;
My heart shall rejoice in Your salvation.
I will sing to the LORD,
Because He has dealt bountifully with me.

PSALM 13:5–6

SCRIPTURE

For He has clothed me with the garments of
    salvation,
He has covered me with the robe of righteousness.

ISAIAH 61:10

PRAYER

Lord, you take my brokenness and replace it with righteousness and salvation. I'm so grateful for this truth, and I'm thankful for your generosity toward me. Please, let me never take your blessings for granted. In Jesus' name, amen.

33

WORSHIP

How precious is Your lovingkindness, O God!
Therefore the children of men put their trust under
the shadow of Your wings.
They are abundantly satisfied with the fullness of
Your house,
And You give them drink from the river of Your
pleasures.
For with You is the fountain of life.

PSALM 36:7–9

SCRIPTURE

But whoever drinks of the water that I shall give
him will never thirst. But the water that I shall
give him will become in him a fountain of water
springing up into everlasting life.

JOHN 4:14

PRAYER

*Dear God, thank you for quenching my thirsty soul with your
living water. When I trust in you, I'm never disappointed. When
I drink from the Water of Life, I am refreshed, renewed, and
restored. Help me turn to you in every stronghold I face. In your
name I pray, amen.*

34

WORSHIP

Come, saints and adore him; come, bow at his feet!
Oh, give him the glory, the praise that is meet;
Let joyful hosannas unceasingly rise,
And join the full chorus that gladdens the skies.

"COME, SAINTS, AND ADORE HIM" BY MARIA DE FLEURY

SCRIPTURE

Do not sorrow, for the joy of the LORD is your
strength.

NEHEMIAH 8:10

PRAYER

Father, I want your joy to be my strength today. When I face an obstacle too big or a stronghold too firm to handle on my own, restore my joy by reminding me of your victory. I worship and praise you because you are my God and I am yours. In Jesus' name, amen.

35

WORSHIP

Make a joyful shout to the LORD, all you lands!
Serve the LORD with gladness;
Come before His presence with singing.
Know that the LORD, He is God;
It is He who has made us, and not we ourselves;
We are His people and the sheep of His pasture.

PSALM 100:1–3

SCRIPTURE

Hear, O Israel: The LORD our God, the LORD is one! You shall love the LORD your God with all your heart, with all your soul, and with all your strength.

DEUTERONOMY 6:4–5

PRAYER

Dear God, you are the one true God. No other "god" can defend me. No idol can save me. With all of my heart, with all of my soul, and with all of my strength, I love you. My heart is filled with gratitude, and it's all yours. In Jesus' name, amen.

36

Worship

Praise the LORD, all you Gentiles!
Laud Him, all you peoples!
For His merciful kindness is great toward us,
And the truth of the LORD endures forever.
Praise the LORD!

PSALM 117:1–2

Scripture

The LORD your God in your midst,
The Mighty One, will save;
He will rejoice over you with gladness,
He will quiet you with His love,
He will rejoice over you with singing.

ZEPHANIAH 3:17

Prayer

Father, I praise you. I thank you. You are truth. When everything else in my life is unreliable, you remain true to your promises. I wake up joyful knowing that I'm covered by your merciful kindness. Because of Christ, I get to spend eternity with you. In Christ I pray, amen.

37

WORSHIP

I will lift up my eyes to the hills—
From whence comes my help?
My help comes from the Lord,
Who made heaven and earth.

PSALM 121:1–2

SCRIPTURE

We may boldly say: "The LORD is my helper; I will not fear. What can man do to me?"

HEBREWS 13:6

PRAYER

Dear God, you help me when I'm in need, and you're a shelter when I'm in trouble. Because you are on my side, I don't have to fear the future. All of my mistakes and failures are forgotten, and you have big plans for me. Thank you, God, for the promise of your protection. In Jesus' name, amen.

38

WORSHIP

My God, how endless is Thy love!
Thy gifts are every evening new;
And morning mercies from above
Gently distill like early dew.

I yield my powers to Thy command,
To Thee I consecrate my days;
Perpetual blessings from Thine hand
Demand perpetual songs of praise.

"MY GOD, HOW ENDLESS IS THY LOVE" BY ISAAC WATTS

SCRIPTURE

The LORD has appeared of old to me, saying:
"Yes, I have loved you with an everlasting love;
Therefore with lovingkindness I have drawn you."

JEREMIAH 31:3

PRAYER

Dear Jesus, your love never fails and it never ends. It is stronger than any sin or stronghold in my life. Your love truly conquers all, and I can come to you at any time because I know I am fully loved, just as I am. In your name, amen.

39

WORSHIP

Praise the Rock of our salvation!
Praise the mighty God above!
Come before His sacred presence
With a grateful song of love.

"PRAISE THE ROCK OF OUR SALVATION" BY FANNY CROSBY

SCRIPTURE

Every good gift and every perfect gift is from
above, and comes down from the Father of lights,
with whom there is no variation or shadow of
turning.

JAMES 1:17

PRAYER

*Dear God, you are great. Every good thing on this earth is from
you. I see your amazing works everywhere I turn—in nature, in
my family, in my friends. Your plans for me are good because all of
your creation is good. Thank you that you never turn your back on
me. In Jesus' name, amen.*

40

WORSHIP

Worship the Lord in the beauty of holiness,
Bow down before Him, His glory proclaim;
Gold of obedience and incense of lowliness,
Bring and adore Him—the Lord is His name.

"WORSHIP THE LORD IN THE BEAUTY OF
HOLINESS" BY JOHN S. B. MONSELL

SCRIPTURE

And not a man of all their enemies stood against
them; the LORD delivered all their enemies into
their hand. Not a word failed of any good thing
which the LORD had spoken to the house of Israel.

JOSHUA 21:44–45

PRAYER

*God, you never fail me. You are true to your word and to your
promises. I worship your holy name, for you are faithful, and you
always have been. You lead me to victory through Jesus, and so it
is in his name I pray this, amen.*

NOTES

Walk Circles Around Your Jericho

1. "Worship of these gods [Baalism] carried with it some of the most demoralizing practices then in existence. Among them were child sacrifice, a practice long since discarded in Egypt and Babylonia, sacred prostitution, and snake-worship on a scale unknown among other peoples." G. Ernest Wright and Floyd V. Filson, *The Westminster Historical Atlas to the Bible* (Philadelphia: Westminster, 1945), 36.

2. Spiros Zodhiates, ed., *Hebrew-Greek Key Word Study Bible: Key Insights into God's Word, New American Standard Bible*, rev. ed. (Chattanooga, TN: AMG Publishers, 2008), #3423, p. 1896.

3. George V. Wigram and Ralph D. Winter, *The Word Study Concordance* (Wheaton, IL: Tyndale, 1972), 477.

4. According to the REVEAL Spiritual Life Survey database 2007–2014, this number is 89 percent. For more information on the REVEAL Survey see Greg L. Hawkins and Cally Parkinson, *Move: What 1,000 Churches Reveal About Spiritual Growth* (Grand Rapids, MI: Zondervan, 2011).

5. Used by permission.

Live Your Promised Land Life Now

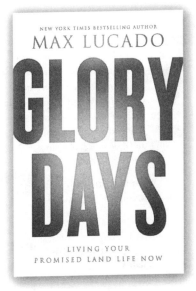

ISBN: 978-0-8499-4849-7
$26.99

You have everything you need to be everything God desires. With God's help you can close the gap between the person you are and the person you want to be.

Available wherever books and ebooks are sold.

GloryDaysBook.com

Tools for your Church and Small Group

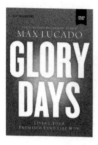

Glory Days: A DVD Study
ISBN: 978-0-7180-3603-4
$ 26.99

Max Lucado leads this six-session study of the book of Joshua and helps modern-day Christians live their Promised Land lives. This study will help small group participants leave fear and worry behind, overcome rejection, and deal with doubt through God's Word.

Glory Days Study Guide
ISBN: 978-0-7180-3597-6
$10.99

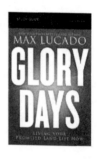

This guide is filled with Scripture study, discussion questions, and practical tools to help small-group members begin living their Promised Land lives now.

Glory Days: Church Campaign Kit
ISBN: 978-0-7180-3598-3
$59.99

The *Glory Days* Church Campaign Kit includes the six-session DVD study by Max Lucado; a study guide with discussion questions and video notes; the *Glory Days* trade book; a getting started guide; and access to all the resources a church needs to launch and sustain this six-week campaign.

Glory Days for Everyone

He Fights for You
ISBN: 978-0-7180-3790-1
$2.99

Includes forty promises featuring worship, Scripture, and guided prayers to face every stronghold in life. It's ideal for churches and ministries to use as an outreach tool.

Glory Days eBook
ISBN: 978-0-7180-3790-1
$27.99

Enjoy *Glory Days* anywhere on your favorite tablet or electronic device.

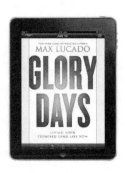

Días de Gloria
Spanish Edition
ISBN: 978-0-7180-3412-2
$13.99

The message of *Glory Days* is also available for Spanish-language readers.

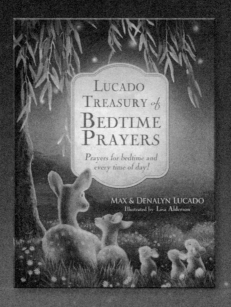